T0131966

A Weekend with

TÜK

Written and Illustrated by
Tamara Devitre Lueders

To order additional copies of this book, contact:
Xlibris
844-714-8691
www.Xlibris.com
Orders@Xlibris.com

ISBN: Softcover   978-1-4257-3028-4

Library of Congress Control Number: 2006907456

Print information available on the last page

Rev. date: 07/09/2021

For

David and Sarah,
as they embark on a new journey
to explore the patterns of life.
September 3, 2006

Hi, my name is TÜK and I am part Great Dane and Labrador and only a year old. One day last week Dad called Grandma to see if she would watch me, while he and Mom went to Michigan for the weekend. Usually I get to go with them to Michigan but this time they flew in an airplane. Grandma hesitantly agreed, and slowly broke the news to Grandpa and the cats.

Friday night, I arrived at Grandma's and Grandpa's with my bed, crate, leash, gentle leader (yuk), toys, bowls, treats and a whole BIG bag of dog food.

While Dad, Mom, Grandma, and Grandpa ate pizza (a bribe so Grandma and Grandpa would keep me), I laid under the dining room table to wait for a hand out. No luck. The next thing I knew, Mom was getting all lovey-dovey with me, walking to the door. Dad said his good-byes and went out to park the car in front of the house. Then Mom followed him. I knew it. They were leaving me again! I started whimpering while I watched them leave with Grandpa for the airport.

Grandma tried to talk to me, but I felt so dejected. Grandma pulled me away from the door and went to sit down on the sofa. I followed her and climbed on the sofa. I looked out the front window and saw Dad's and Mom's empty, dark car. How could they do this to me? I hung my head over the cushions as I looked at the car, and blinked my eyes a few times to keep back the tears.

Grandma tried to comfort me by petting me and telling me how wonderful I am. I tried to relax, but whenever I heard a noise, I looked out the window. The car was still there, but no Dad or Mom.

When Grandpa came back from the airport, the three of us spent the evening on the sofa. Grandma and Grandpa were watching television, while I laid down between them sulking.

That night Grandma felt sorry for me and spent the night in the spare bedroom with me. She read me a story, and even let me cuddle next to her in the bed so I wouldn't have to sleep alone in the crate. Grandpa slept with their two cats. The cats don't like me to go in Grandma's and Grandpa's room. Actually, they don't like me very much, at all. That's okay though, I got to sleep with Grandma.

The next morning Grandma and Grandpa had to go out. They wanted me to go in the crate in the bedroom. I just knew they were leaving me, too, when they put on their jackets.

"TÜK, treat!" Grandma said while she dangled the dog biscuit in front of my nose.

At first I played innocent. I thought, "Who me? Me, get off the sofa?"

"TÜK, treat!"

Man, it works every time. I have to have more self- control, but some treats are worth it. I went to the crate. Then Grandma gave me my treat. Next thing I heard was CLICK, CLICK, the locking of the crate.

"Good boy," they said and left.

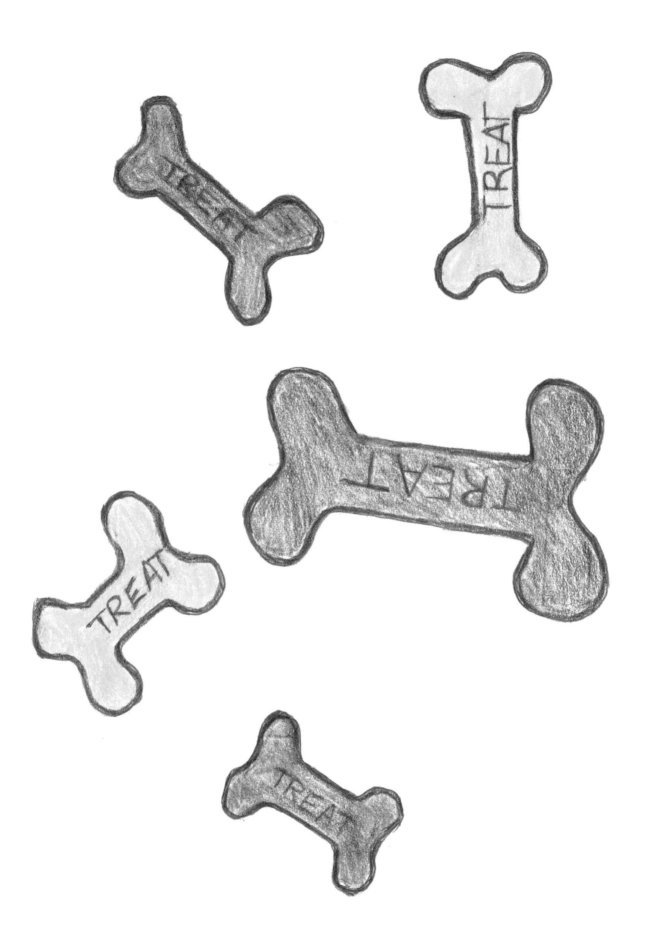

CLICK, CLICK

When they got home, Grandma was going to take me for a walk. She got her walking clothes on and came to me with the gentle leader. I was so excited to go for a walk, but not with the gentle leader! Now, she just had to know how I felt about it. I started jumping, shaking the floor, making Grandma's glassware clink together in the dining room!

I barked, "WOOF, WOOF, WOOF!" (I won't wear it!) "WOOF, WOOF, WOOF!" Okay, I think she understood. She went back to the kitchen, to get more treats and a couple of poop bags. Her pockets were bulging with treats! Now she's talking! Grandpa and Grandma put the gentle leader and leash on me. Grandpa walked us out the door and waved. Grandma and I walked four blocks. It was fun smelling each and every road sign, fire hydrant, tree, bush, mailbox post, utility pole, and rock on the way and back. When we got back home we took a nap.

The cats kept hiding from me but Grandpa has some real weird toys that move all by themselves, maybe I can play with them. This ant of his dances and sings. I think it's crazy or something. I started jumping at it, shaking the floor, and BARKING like a mad dog. Grandma had to put it up on the piano before I chewed its head off.

Grandpa's remote control car has really big wheels, flashing lights, makes a loud whirring sound, and is hard to catch. When I do catch it, the wheels turn in my mouth. It makes me BARK, then it jumps out of my mouth! I looked at Grandpa. He was laughing really hard. I gave him one of my looks. "Stop pushing those buttons, Grandpa!"

There is one more thing at their house that is r-e-a-l-l-y SCARY! Usually things are afraid of me because of my BIG size and my FEROCIOUS bark and my sharp POINTED teeth. Yet, nothing bothers their pet alligator, Okie. No matter how hard I made the floor shake, the windows rattle, or many things fall off the shelf, the gator wasn't afraid of me. It just sat there! Once in a while it would move toward me with its mouth open wide, teeth looking as SHARP as mine, showing its long, red tongue. It would throw me into such a tizzy fit, I kept barking and banging into the furniture to show it my teeth were as SHARP as its teeth. My tail was just as long as its tail. Wait a minute. . . . . my tongue is pink . . . . . the gator's tongue is red. Something seems fishy.

Gators don't have red tongues! Okie even smells strange, like oily rubber!

I looked at Grandpa. He was laughing. I gave him one of those looks. "Grandpa take your hands off that gator! You are playing games with me again!"

Saturday night, I was so tired from messing with the gator. When Grandma and Grandpa got ready to go out without me, I settled down in my crate with the big bone Grandma gave me. They are getting better with these treats. I think they are finally getting the hang of it. Getting treats like that, who cares about self-control and letting them win! CLICK, CLICK.

"Good boy TÜK!" they said.

TREAT

TREAT

TREAT

TREAT

TREAT

CLICK, CLICK

A few hours later, I heard them unlock the front door, and started to wag my tail.

"Hi TÜK!" Grandma said. CLICK, CLICK. Man, I bolted out of the crate, jumped up on her, practically knocking her down!

She said frantically, "WAIT, WAIT, TÜK!" and scrambled for the back door to let me out. Man, I was so happy to see her I couldn't stop jumping and barking! When we came back in I still wanted to play but she wanted to sleep. I gave in and laid down beside her, but with my head hanging over the edge of the bed hoping one of the cats might accidentally stroll by.

When morning came, Grandma and Grandpa took me for a LONG walk. After a few treats, the gentle leader went on fine. On the way home Grandma couldn't keep up with us and our long legs. Every once in awhile I'd stop and see if she was okay. Grandpa and I would wait until she caught up with us.

Grandpa is my pal now, too bad, cats. I forgive him for teasing me about the ant, car, and gator. We just hung out like a couple of couch potatoes watching the football game. I am not sure which one of us fell asleep first.

Later I heard Grandma stirring in the kitchen and got up to see what she was doing. She got my ball out of the bag and took me outside. I started playing with her when all of a sudden, "YAP, YAP, YAP!" It was their new neighbor's dogs barking at the fence. Naturally, I had to go meet them and let them know what my bark sounded like and who I was. We dogs ran along opposite sides of the fence, jumping and barking, until other dogs in the neighborhood joined us in making noise. Then I marked my new friend next door. I wanted the other dog to know that Bam Bam was MY new friend. Grandma was shocked and made me come in after that.

Grandpa left to pick up Mom and Dad from the airport. Grandma was about out of tricks and sat down at the piano. When she started playing it and singing, I bolted upright! I am not sure whether it was the playing or singing that really got to me, but you know what came next. "WOOF, WOOF, WOOF!" She played high notes and she played low notes. "WOOF, WOOF, WOOF!"

She started laughing and saying, "Oh TÜK, you sing so well. Why don't you come and play the piano with me, too?" That's all I needed to hear. I went hurriedly over to Grandma's left side and laid my jaw on the keys. BWAM! Grandma thought it was so cute, she tried to get me to do it again. Man, I had enough of that! My rubber chicken was calling me, at least it couldn't squawk in my ears anymore like the piano.

Grandma went over to the sofa to sit down. I decided to join her. After I got comfortable, I heard a noise outside. Then I saw lights. Grandpa drove in the driveway.

"Hey, wait a minute," I thought, "someone is getting out of the car, no two people. Could it be..... they are going over to Dad's car?" My tail started to wag, my butt started moving from side to side. I hurried to the door with Grandma. I tried to push the door open. It wouldn't budge. Finally, Grandma opened it. I jumped as high as Mom and Dad are tall! I kept jumping and barking! I was so excited, I love them SOOOO much! They were just as happy to see me! They hugged me and kissed me! I licked all over their faces and kept jumping up on them!

Grandma and Grandpa told Mom and Dad about our weekend together. The gentle leader, the walks, sleeping with Grandma, the story, playing with the car, the ant, the ugly gator, the dogs next door, the cats, the toys, and my ability to BWAM the piano made up for a busy weekend.

I'll never forget that weekend with Grandma and Grandpa. When I got home, I slept like a baby.

My dad said, "Yep, TÜK you must have had a good time!" Mom agreed.

Meanwhile back at Grandma's and Grandpa's house, the cats came out from hiding, and things returned to normal. They all slept well that night.

A Weekend with

Printed in the United States
by Baker & Taylor Publisher Services